Podcasting Essentials

Start, Record, and Monetize Your Way to Stardom

Table of Contents

Chapter 1. Introduction

Dive into the exciting world of podcasting with our Special Report: "Podcasting Essentials: Start, Record, and Monetize Your Way to Stardom". Amidst an era when voices are becoming as impactful as words, we simplify the art of podcasting down to its very essence, making it engaging, informative and fun! This vibrant guide will walk you through the key stepping stones - starting your very own podcast, recording with crystal-clear quality, and shaping ingenious strategies to monetize your creative endeavor. Podcasting novices and enthusiasts, now is your chance to uncap the secrets of podcasting stardom. Empower your voice, exhilarate your listeners, and embrace an enthralling odyssey towards becoming an influential podcaster! By the time you're done with this report, you might just be pressing 'Record' on your first episode. Now, doesn't that sound like music to your ears? Tune in, and let's create awe-inspiring audio content together!

Chapter 2. Understanding the Podcasting Landscape

The ever-evolving landscape of the podcasting world presents a plethora of opportunities and challenges. It has become a dynamic tool for individuals, businesses, and organizations to express ideas, share stories, and give insights into different fields. The global expansion of this platform has become instrumental in shaping how information and ideas are consumed.

For a neophyte stepping into the gears of podcasting, understanding the vast expanse of this terrain is the first and foremost task; from grasping its history to visualizing its tremendous growth, apprehending the diverse categories, recognizing the trends, and finally, comprehending its future implications.

2.1. A Brief History of Podcasting

The world was introduced to the concept of podcasting – a concatenation of iPod and broadcast – back in 2004. Proposed by Dave Slusher and endorsed by Adam Curry and Dave Slusher, this term revolutionized the audio content industry. While internet radio broadcasts had been around for a while, the concept of a podcast allowed listeners to consume radio-style content on their own time, unchained from live schedules.

As technology advanced, so did podcasting. Apple's support from 2005 amplified the podcasting wave, with it becoming a mainstream digital content platform in the years to follow. With the technological boom in the late 2000s to early 2010s, podcasting proliferated faster and more extensively, reaching audiences across the globe.

2.2. Categories in Podcasting

Just like a library bookshelf, the podcasting realm is packed with a myriad of categories, each with its unique charm. News and politics, health and wellness, true crime, arts, business, comedy, and education are among the prominent ones.

Within the business genre, subcategories like entrepreneurship, marketing, management, and finance each garner sizable listeners. Comedy podcasts, unscripted and full of banter, can lighten your day, while true crime podcasts with their dramatic narratives and investigative storytelling captivate and thrill. Health and wellness podcasts cater to mental, physical, and spiritual health devotees. The categories are as broad and diverse as the potential podcasting audience.

2.3. Understanding Current Podcasting Trends

In the ever-changing tech-based world, following trends gives you an edge. Podcast listeners mostly consist of the younger population. With a rising trend towards mobile consumption, it's prevalent to see portable devices being the primary medium for podcast enjoyment.

Another trend is multitasking; people are more likely to listen to a podcast while performing routine tasks. Serialization of content, just as we see on television and in novels, is yet another trend in the podcasting world, and it works wonders for retention and ongoing engagement.

Moreover, businesses and organizations are leaping into the podcasting bandwagon. Podcasts are becoming essential strategic communication tools for businesses geared toward brand promotion, knowledge sharing, and establishing thought leadership.

2.4. The Future of Podcasting

Envisioning the future of podcasting, three primary aspects could shape its course - technology, monetization, and content direction. As technology evolves with the advent of 5G, artificial intelligence, and more, a richer and more interactive podcasting experience is on the horizon.

Monetization avenues are also likely to expand beyond conventional advertising and sponsorships; crowdfunding, community-led payments, and more will gain more prominence. And content-wise, niche podcasts will continue to grow, appealing to specific classes of interest.

2.5. Navigating the Podcasting Landscape

Finally, navigating through this vast landscape requires strategic planning. You must be adept at recognizing the prevalent trends and using them to your advantage. The choice of category should resonate with your passion and knowledge, drawing its energy from your personal authenticity.

Understanding the diversity of listeners and their preference is key. It's essential to create content that appeals to your target audience, employing an engaging narrative style, choosing a compelling topic that resonates, and maintaining a consistent delivery pattern.

Moreover, aligning with technology by being open to new platforms, tools, and trends can cater to a broader and more tech-savvy audience. Lastly, striving towards continuous learning and development, and being committed to innovation and creativity can equip you to ride the podcasting wave with confidence and command.

Thus, equipped with a clear understanding of the podcasting landscape, you are now ready to embark on the fascinating journey of sharing your voice and ideas with the world!

Chapter 3. Creating Riveting Content: Your Unique Voice

The enchanting world of podcasting opens its arms to a vast range of topics and niches. It allows you to let your creativity run wild, engaging with your audience in a myriad of ways. Podcasters can pick up from art to zoology, and everything in between, showcasing their expertise, perspective and unique voice. However, to transform from a mere podcast enthusiast to an influential podcaster, the key lies in creating riveting content. Here, we explore the process, techniques, and strategies to help you find your unique voice and captivate your audience with mesmerizing stories and insightful conversations.

3.1. Discovering Your Unique Voice

Your voice is more than just the sound you generate. It signifies your personality, your perspectives, and your passion. To discover your unique voice, start by identifying your interests or a subject matter about which you're most passionate or knowledgeable. It could be anything from entrepreneurship, environmental issues, history, science fiction to crochet, gardening, and cooking.

Next, understand your strengths. Are you good at conducting interviews? Do you explain complex topics in easy-to-understand ways? Or do you craft mesmerizing stories? Identifying your strengths will help shape your content and make it stand out.

Show authenticity. Your listeners tune in to your podcasts not just because of the topic; they want to hear your unique perspective. So, don't shy away from sharing your personal experiences and opinions. Authenticity breeds trust, which is essential in fostering a loyal listenership.

3.2. Creating Engaging Content

With your voice defined and your theme decided, it's time to start creating engaging content. A well-structured podcast with a clear flow helps listeners stay invested in your content.

Every episode should have a beginning, a middle, and an end. The beginning or the introduction is your opportunity to catch your listener's attention. Give them a glimpse of what they should expect in the episode. The middle delivers the main content. This is where your unique voice should shine. Lastly, the conclusion allows you to summarize your points and share a call-to-action like asking your listeners to subscribe or share your podcast.

Make your content actionable. This means providing your listeners with specific actions they can take based on what they've just heard. Actionable content can increase engagement, encourage listenership, and strengthen audience connection.

3.3. Mastering the Art of Storytelling

Effective storytelling is one of the most powerful tools you can wield in podcasting. Stories are relatable, evoke emotions, and make your content memorable. Drawing from personal experiences or real-world examples can make your storytelling more impactful.

Dig deeper into the subject matter. Going beyond the surface level can provide your audience with a fresh perspective and inspire them to think differently. This not only positions you as a knowledgeable source but also grips your audience with intriguing, thoughtful content.

3.4. Crafting an Attractive Title

The title of your podcast episode is the first impression. It should be intriguing enough to capture the listener's attention and reflective of the content. Play around with humor, puns, or gripping questions. Use compelling language that sparks curiosity and resonates with your target audience.

3.5. Enhancing Your Podcast With Visuals

Although podcasting is an auditory medium, you can enhance its reach by using graphics or visual aids. Creating striking cover arts and episode thumbnails can significantly improve visibility on podcast platforms. Moreover, visuals also help when promoting your podcast on various social media platforms.

3.6. Reacting to Feedback and Adjusting Accordingly

Continuous improvement is an important part of creating riveting content. Delight in the praise, but also graciously accept criticism. Let your audience's feedback guide your future episodes. This is not only a great way to boost listener engagement but also ensure your podcast content continually evolves and stays relevant.

Remember, your voice lights the way for your podcast's success. Be brave. Be bold. Be you. The more time you spend honing your unique voice, the more confidently it will ring out in your podcasting journey and captivate listeners from all walks of life. Use this guide as a starting point and refine it as you evolve into a pro podcaster, sharing your unique voice and story with the world. Isn't that the most beautiful and thrilling part of this journey? This is your microphone. Now, let your voice shine!

Chapter 4. Tackling Podcast Technology: Tools and Equipment

Before embarking on the journey of podcasting, one crucial consideration is the technology behind it. It's the backbone that ensures the smooth running of your show and contributes to capturing your voice in the best possible light.

We will dive into the world of podcast technology, casting a spotlight on necessary tools and equipment and how to use them efficiently.

4.1. Microphones

Arguably the most significant piece of equipment you'll need is a quality microphone. While it's possible to record a podcast using your smartphone or laptop's built-in microphone, a dedicated microphone can dramatically improve the quality of your recordings. Various types of microphones suit different needs:

- **Dynamic Microphones**: Ideal for beginners due to their affordability and durability. They're less sensitive to surrounding noises making them suited for podcasters who might be recording in less-than-ideal environments.

- **Condenser Microphones**: These are more expensive, deliver exceptional audio quality but capture more background noises. Ideal for studio setups.

- **USB Microphones**: These are plug-and-play microphones, perfect for those who want ease and simplicity. While they might not offer the best audio quality, they are certainly adequate for fledgling podcasters.

- **XLR Microphones**: Generally considered professional-tier microphones, they require more setup and an audio interface for connection but offer exceptional audio.

4.2. Headphones

Quality headphones are essential for podcasting. They enable you to monitor the audio quality in real-time during recording and aid in the editing process. Opt for closed-back headphones as they are excellent for sound isolation, ensuring that what you hear is just what's in the podcast without ambient noise interference.

4.3. Audio Interface

An audio interface connects your microphone to your computer and vastly improves the audio quality compared to a direct connection. It also gives you precision control over input gain, and with most interfaces, it enables you to connect multiple microphones, something essential if you plan on having guests or a co-host.

4.4. Pop Filters and Microphone Stands

To cut back on those pesky 'popping' sounds that come from 'p', 'b', and 't' sounds, you'll need a pop filter. Besides, a good microphone stand not only keeps your mic secure but if you get a boom arm stand it can reduce handling noise.

4.5. Podcast Hosting & Distribution Platforms

Once you've recorded your podcast, you'll need somewhere to host it. Hosting platforms store your podcast files and create RSS feeds, which podcast directories and apps utilize to distribute your podcast. There are several hosting platforms, like Libsyn, Podbean, and Anchor, to name a few.

Beyond the initial hosting, you also need to distribute your podcast to podcast directories and apps like Apple Podcasts, Spotify, Google Podcasts, and many others. Some hosting platforms automate this process, taking much of the complexity out of distribution.

4.6. Recording & Editing Software

Respectively called DAWs (Digital Audio Workstations), recording and editing software is where you will spend a significant amount of time shaping your podcast. Popular choices include Audacity (free), GarageBand (free for Apple users), Adobe Audition, and more premium DAWs like Logic Pro X.

Each comes with its unique range of features, but fundamentally they allow you to record, import audio, cut, paste, edit, add effects, and mix multiple tracks.

4.7. Soundproofing

Although not equipment precisely, soundproofing is a part of your physical setup that can drastically affect the quality of your podcast. For optimal audio, you need a quiet, echo-free environment. But soundproofing a room costs money and can be overkill. Using a dynamic microphone (as mentioned before) can reduce background noise considerably. Other "do-it-yourself" and budget-friendly solutions include recording in a closet (clothes insulate sound), hanging heavy drapes or blankets, and using foam panels.

4.8. Portable Equipment

Mobile podcasting equipment like portable recorders and XLR-to-USB adapters allows you to record quality podcasts on the go. Be ready to capture the moment wherever you are, making your podcast unique.

4.9. Monetization Plugins and Tools

Once your podcast is up and running, you might start thinking about monetization. Tools like Patreon, Ko-fi, or memberful allow you to set up subscription services, while dynamic ad insertion platforms like PodAds offer opportunities to insert ads into your podcast automatically.

Now that we've gone over the equipment and technology necessary for podcasting, you're well on your way to starting your own podcast! Each podcaster may have different needs, and it's essential to keep those in mind when making purchasing decisions. Remember, podcasting is not just about the best gear, but also about content and making a connection with your audience. Invest in what you need instead of getting caught up in owning the latest and the best.

From there, you'll want to focus on actually producing your podcast. Keep in mind, the importance of good sound should not be underestimated; it is outweighed only perhaps by the quality of the content. Focus on delivering value through your content and the sound that carries it!

Chapter 5. Mastering the Art of Audio Recording

The journey towards creating a successful podcast begins with understanding the fundamental elements of audio recording. A clear, crisp and well-balanced audio production not only ensures listener satisfaction, but anchors your credibility as a podcaster. However, fret not if this phrase rings a bell of uncertainty, because we're here to unravel all ambiguities, taking you from dilettante to connoisseur.

5.1. Acquainting With Audio Basics

First and foremost, let's familiarize ourselves with a few key terminologies. 'Sample rate' refers to the number of samples per unit of time taken from a continuous signal to make a discrete signal. Ideally, the minimum sample rate should be 44.1 kHz for acceptable quality. 'Bit depth', in simpler terms, is the amount of data included in each sample, which in turn reflects the dynamic range of an audio file. 16 bits is typically sufficient for podcast recording.

5.2. The Emergence of the 'Golden Trio': The Microphone, Audio Interface, and Headphones

The right equipment plays an intrinsic role in capturing excellent audio. This golden trio - microphone, audio interface, and headphones - forms the trinity of quality podcasting. Microphones convert sound waves into an electrical signal, audio interfaces further refine this signal for recording, while headphones grant you the ability to closely monitor your audio quality and nuances.

Choosing a microphone for podcasts can seem daunting, given the range of models and types available. The most common types are dynamic and condenser microphones. Dynamic microphones are robust, generally cheaper, and offer good overall sound quality, making them ideal for beginners. Condenser microphones, meanwhile, offer superior sound quality and sensitivity, but are more expensive and delicate.

An audio interface, often overlooked by beginners, bridges the gap between your microphone and your computer. Quality is important here – a better interface will offer higher sample rates and bit depths, translating to superior audio quality.

Lastly, the ideal pair of headphones for podcasting gives you a balanced sound output, rather than bass-heavy music headphones. Seek out closed-back headphones for best results as they minimize bleed into the microphone when recording.

5.3. Getting Acquainted with Recording Software

Once you have the golden trio set, it's time to pick your recording software. Often referred to as Digital Audio Workstations (DAWs), these programs allow you to record, edit, and mix your podcast episodes. Some popular DAWs amongst podcasters are Audacity, GarageBand (for Mac users), and Adobe Audition.

Audacity is a free, open-source DAW, making it a common choice for beginners. It offers a range of editing tools and supports multiple plugins. GarageBand, for Apple users, is also free and user-friendly, brimming with a wealth of sound effects and music loops. Adobe Audition is a professional-grade DAW, with podcasters lauding its noise reduction capabilities, ease of use, and powerful editing tools.

5.4. Right Recording Technique and Environment

A seldom-discussed aspect of audio recording is technique and environment. Start off by ensuring a quiet and echo-free room. Soft surfaces absorb sound, so placing curtains, rugs or padded foam panels can significantly reduce echo. Your speaking technique also matters - be mindful of your distance from the microphone, your speaking volume, and the angle of the microphone.

5.5. Editing and Post-Production

In the final stage of recording, editing and post-production can elevate your podcast to professional standards. This process entails cutting unnecessary portions, adjusting volume levels, removing background noise, and arranging segments. When done successfully, post-production refines your podcast, resulting in smooth and enjoyable listening.

While there's a learning curve involved, patience, practice, and persistence in post-production reaps tremendous rewards. Remember, in podcasting, your voice is your brand. Ensuring pristine audio quality is akin to curating a distinct brand image, one that captures listeners and magnifies your reach.

5.6. Conclusion

Mastering audio recording is a pivotal step in your podcasting journey. With a solid understanding of the fundamentals, the right equipment, precise technique and calculated post-production efforts, you lay the bedrock for a high-quality podcast. Once you've grasped these elements, the microphone is your oyster, and the world, your audience.

As you navigate your podcast venture, remember that every renowned podcaster was once a novice. So, plunge into the vibrant world of podcasting, experiment, make mistakes, learn, and most importantly, have fun. The exhilarating moment when you press 'record' for the first time symbolizes not just the birth of a podcast, but the inception of a journey, a journey where your voice holds the power to inspire, enlighten, and entertain.

Chapter 6. Shaping Your Podcast Identity: Branding and Design

Your podcast serves as a reflection of you and your brand. Creating a distinguishing identity that sets you apart is thus paramount. This process starts with the crucial step of shaping your podcast's branding and design – from selecting a suitable name and developing an eye-catching logo to crafting a compelling description for your podcast series.

6.1. Creating a Unique Podcast Name

A name holds power. It can provoke curiosity, clearly relay your podcast's theme, or even provide a chuckle if you choose to encompass humor. But most importantly, it should be remarkable – instinctive enough for your podcast to be recollected amongst the thousands available online.

First off, always prioritize clarity over complexity. Podcast names should be distinct and clear, thus avoiding any potential misunderstandings from your target listeners. Do not engulf your podcast name in jargon or clever plays on words that only a distinct subgroup of individuals will appreciate.

It's a good method to incorporate keywords relevant to your podcast's theme into the title. For instance, if your podcast covers financial advice, including terms like 'wealth', 'finance', or 'investment' can be beneficial for listeners searching for that particular type of content. Although remember, inundating your title with too many keywords can look spammy and may deter potential listeners.

Finally, shorter names are more memorable. They're easier to share verbally and take up less space on podcast directories. Try keeping your podcast name under four to five words. However, this isn't a hard and fast rule. If a longer name suits your podcast's theme and tone better, then don't balk from it.

6.2. Designing a Captivating Podcast Logo

The next major component of your podcast identity is the visual design, often distilled into a single main element – your podcast logo. This will be the first element many potential listeners observe while browsing through various podcasts online. Therefore, spending time and resources on a professional-looking design is well worth it.

Your logo should rapidly communicate your podcast's tone and theme and should be discernible even at a smaller size since podcast logos often appear thumbnail-sized on most platforms. Therefore, using simple, bold designs with high-contrast colors can help your logo stand out amongst others.

Text within the logo should be minimized, but if necessary, should be clear and legible. Remember, though – your podcast's name will be next to the logo in all directories, eliminating the need for repetitive text.

Copying and inspiration are two different things. Feel free to seek inspiration from successful podcast logos but avoid duplication. Your logo should be unique, communicating your podcast's personality and making it instantly identifiable.

6.3. Writing a Compelling Podcast Description

A podcast description or summary serves as your elevator pitch to potential listeners, quickly communicating what your podcast is about and why they should listen. A captivating description could be the deciding factor in a potential listener clicking 'play' on your podcast or scrolling past it.

Remember to communicate your unique value proposition clearly. What will the listeners gain from tuning into your podcast? What makes your podcast different from others discussing similar topics? Answering these questions in your description will entice potential listeners.

Detailed descriptions can improve your visibility online. Podcast platforms often use algorithms that scan for keywords in descriptions to match search queries. So, if you're producing a podcast on climate change, incorporating words and phrases related to environmental issues, sustainability, global warming, renewable energy, etc., can boost your chances of being discovered.

However, resist the temptation to overload your description with keywords. Trying to game the algorithm can lead to awkwardly worded descriptions that turn listeners off.

6.4. Developing Your Podcast's Audio Branding

Your audio branding consists of aspects like your podcast's intro and outro music, any recurring audio motifs, and even the kind of language and tonality you adopt. These elements combine to create a unique sound associated with your podcast, enhancing its recall value.

For intro and outro music, use something that matches the energy and tone of your podcast. High-tempo music can set an energetic, fast-paced tone, while slower rhythms might be more suitable for relaxed, conversational podcasts. Original music compositions are ideal to avoid copyright issues, but royalty-free music is a budget-friendly alternative.

Recurring audio elements, like sound effects or specific phrases, also contribute to your podcast's audio branding. Consistency is key – using the same elements in every episode makes your podcast instantly recognizable.

The kind of language and tone you use can speak volumes about your podcast. If your content is high-brow and intellectual, using sophisticated vocabulary might add value. However, for most podcasts, using accessible, conversational language fosters a sense of connection and inclusivity.

In conclusion, shaping your podcast identity is an elaborate task that involves careful thought and planning. However, remember that a podcast should always be a true representation of yourself and the message you want to convey to the world. Be distinct, be true, and create with promise and passion, and your podcast will surely strike a chord with listeners.

Chapter 7. Engaging Your Audience: Promotion and Outreach

Engaging your audience effectively is the veritable golden ticket to the land of flourishing podcasting. It's vital not necessarily because it helps you gather more listeners, but because it helps you gather the 'right' listeners—the ones who will make it a point to tune into every episode you upload and leave enthralled, positive reviews that beckon other listeners.

7.1. Identifying Your Target Audience

Before embarking on this journey of audience engagement, it's crucial you identify 'who' your listeners will be. Imagine your perfect listener. What are their interests, age, location, and hobbies? Start considering the finer nuances like their preferred podcast length and preferred listening time. The more you understand your audience, the more streamlined your promotional strategies can become. Gather insights, analyze demographics, and uncover your listener archetype to create content that resonates with them and fosters a powerful and enduring relationship.

7.2. Understanding Your Value Proposition

People tune into podcasts looking for some value. The value may be in the form of entertainment, education, introspective discussions, or even light-hearted banter. Understanding what makes your podcast unique or worthwhile for a listener is imperative. This understanding grants you the power to articulate your uniqueness in audience engagements, making it simpler for listeners to see why they should tune in to your podcast over the countless others.

7.3. Building Your Brand Identity

Just as businesses need strong branding to set themselves apart, your podcast too needs a recognizable brand identity. This identity is not merely your logo or podcast name, but it encompasses the kind of content you put forth, how you put it, your web presence, your episode naming schedule, and much more. The more polished and consistent your brand identity, the greater is your chance of fostering loyal listenership.

7.4. Leveraging Social Media Platforms

Social media platforms are powerful tools in your audience engagement arsenal. But rather than have a passive presence on every platform, identify which platforms your potential listeners are most active on. Now focus your energy on creating engaging content for these platforms. Go beyond just promoting your new episodes—an effective social media strategy is about creating conversations, facilitating interactions, and fostering a community. This community subsequently becomes your loyal listener base.

7.5. Running Contests or Giveaways

Contests and giveaways can be an exciting way to engage your audience. Not only do they provide interactive opportunities, but they also can aid in widening your listener base. You may request contestants to share your podcast on their social media profiles or tag their friends. In exchange for such actions, provide them a chance to win an exclusive bonus episode, a shout-out in an episode, or even merchandise.

7.6. Collaborating with Other Podcasters

Just as the old saying goes, "Two heads are better than one," the same applies in the podcasting sphere. By collaborating with other podcasters, you widen your reach to include their listener base. Additionally, their listeners might find additional value and shared interests, thus fueling engagement and possibly even gaining you new subscribers. Collaborations could include guest episodes, joint segments, or social media takeover days.

7.7. Creating a Professional Website

Despite the rapidly evolving world of web platforms, having your own comprehensive and professional-looking website still stands as an anchor for your online presence. Here, your listeners can access all your episodes, read transcripts, explore additional resources, and also engage with you or other listeners directly through comments or forums. A 'Subscribe' button or news-feed registration option can also ensure that your listeners keep returning for more.

7.8. Engaging Listeners Through Email Newsletters

Speaking of returning listeners, email newsletters can be a surprisingly effective channel to engage your audience intimately. Regular newsletters with episode highlights, behind-the-scenes snippets, or even your personal thoughts can give your listeners an additional layer of engagement. Whilst it's key not to spam, pertinent and appealing content through emails can foster a closely-knit listener community.

7.9. Staying Consistent

Remember that you are playing the long game. Audience engagement is not about bursts of interest followed by spells of silence. Be consistent with your content release, listener interaction, social media activity, and responsiveness. Building trust and rapport with your audience is a marathon, not a sprint. And as you stay dedicated and consistent, slowly but surely, you'll see your podcast burgeon into an influential and beloved platform—a sweet symphony in the world of podcasting!

7.10. Measuring Your Audience Engagement

Last but not least, always look at your podcasting journey as a learning curve. Use analytics and insights to ascertain if your strategies are successful, or if changes need to be made. Are more listeners tuning in? Is your social media followers count increasing? Are you getting more positive reviews? Balance your intuitive understanding of your audience with analytical data for optimal results.

Podcasting offers a profound and rewarding journey where you can connect with thousands through your unique voice. Be genuine, be patient, and be adaptable. Remember, the heart of an engaging podcast lies not in attracting an audience, but in captivating their attention and hearts through your insightful and resonant content. Your path to podcasting stardom awaits, take your step today!

Chapter 8. The Power of Networking in Podcasting

In the world of podcasting, building a robust network is as crucial as great content or high-end technology. Networking opens doors that can transform your podcast from a fun side project to a full-on career. Here, we'll examine the importance of networking, how to approach it, and a wealth of strategies to make it fruitful.

8.1. The Essence of Networking in Podcasting

Before we get to the nuts and bolts of networking, let's first understand its essence. Networking involves building and nurturing relationships that further your podcast's reach and help propel it towards success. These relationships can be with fellow podcasters, expert guests, industry leaders, fans, or sponsors.

Each connection adds value to your podcast, whether it's through cross-promotion, gaining knowledge and advice, sourcing exciting guests, or finding financial support. Beyond that, a supportive network provides a sense of community and motivation. It reminds you that you are not alone in your podcasting journey.

8.2. Broadening Your Circle and the Concept of Cross-Promotion

Cross-promotion is a beneficial product of networking. This encompasses everything from guesting on each other's shows, shout-outs in episodes, to mentions in newsletters or social media platforms.

Actively collaborate with fellow podcasters who share the same niche. This way, you expose your content to a broader audience who are already interested in similar topics. Not only does this give your podcast a visibility boost, it also fosters a sense of camaraderie among podcasters in your niche.

8.3. Sourcing Exciting Guests

Guests can bring substantial value to your podcast, providing expert insights, different viewpoints, or just an exciting dynamic. Quality guests also attract more listeners, as fans will tune in for their favorite experts or public figures.

Building relationships with potential guests is key. Attend events, contact them directly, or utilize social media. Remember to genuinely express your appreciation of their work and clarify how their presence on your show can be mutually beneficial.

8.4. Courting Sponsors and Advertisers

Monetizing your podcast often involves securing sponsorship from businesses. A network of sponsors and advertisers can provide a steady income stream to help improve and sustain your podcasting endeavor.

Create a media kit presenting your podcast's unique selling points, listener demographics, and download stats. Reach out to brands whose ethos aligns with your content. Maintain communication, stay attentive to their expectations, and deliver on your promises to nurture these valuable relationships.

8.5. Fan Interaction and Community Building

Your listener base is perhaps the most crucial aspect of your network. Engaging and interacting with your audience can create a loyal and active community around your podcast.

This connection can be facilitated by leveraging social media groups, mailing lists, or virtual and physical meetups. Regular interaction can provide a valuable feedback loop and cultivate a sense of ownership among the listeners, which in turn improves content and boosts audience growth.

8.6. Relationship Management and Maintenance

Just like personal relationships, professional connections take time and effort to cultivate and maintain. Regular check-ins, mutual collaborations, and showing up for others can go a long way in preserving and strengthening these bonds.

Be authentic in your interactions. Genuine relationships are always more rewarding and enduring than transactional ones. Remember, what you get out of networking depends greatly on what you put in.

To conclude, the power of networking in podcasting cannot be overstated. Building a robust, dynamic network is essential for growth, monetization, and enriching your podcasting journey. It provides a gateway to collaborative endeavors, invaluable advice, insightful guests, and loyal listeners. Networking is the heartbeat of the podcasting community, fueling its continuous evolution and maintaining its vibrant pulse.

Chapter 9. Monetizing Your Podcast: Strategies and Opportunities

Delving into the podcast business, one quickly realizes how the medium lends itself to various modes of monetization. Channels for revenue generation are no longer confined to standard advertising models or sponsorships, but rather present a vast and intriguing landscape brimming with creative and profitable possibilities.

9.1. Creating Valuable Content

The first rule of monetizing your podcast starts with creating valuable content. Given the abundance of free content available today, it is no wonder audiences balk at the thought of parting with their hard-earned money for mere information. The secret lies in promising enraptured listeners something that few others can rival - content that is relevant, engaging, unique, and consistently delivered.

Aim for creating high-quality content that encapsulates important insights for your audience. It could mean interviewing industry influencers, sharing your own professional knowledge, or making your listeners privy to best-kept secrets. Breathtaking storylines and impactful content are your best bet to retain your listeners and pique their interest.

9.2. Advertisements and Sponsorships

Now, let's tackle a reliable source of revenue — advertisements and sponsorships. Both work on the principle of leveraging your listener base and content to promote a relevant product or service.

Direct advertisements involve short, promotional ad spots within your podcast where you endorse a product or service. These can be instituted at the beginning (pre-roll), middle (mid-roll), or end (post-roll) of your episode. The CPM (cost per mille/thousand) model is most frequently employed here, where payment is per thousand listeners.

Sponsorships, on the other hand, inculcate a deeper engagement between the podcaster and the advertiser. A sponsorship involves more than mere product promotion - it incorporates the sponsor's offerings into the show's content naturally and authentically, making it more appealing to the listeners.

9.3. Listener Contributions

Another strategy to consider is soliciting direct support from your listeners through patronage platforms like Patreon, Buy Me A Coffee, or even crowdfunding websites. These platforms let your listeners make regular contributions or one-off donations to support your podcast. In return, they usually receive rewards like bonus content, merchandise, or shout-outs.

9.4. Premium Content and Subscriptions

Offering premium content for a subscription fee or pay-per-episode charge has also gained popularity. This can be additional content, ad-free episodes, early access to new releases, or bonus material like PDFs or video content related to your podcast.

Moreover, with platforms such as Apple Podcast Subscriptions and Spotify's paid podcast program, it's now easier than ever for podcasters to introduce subscription models for their listeners.

9.5. Merchandising

Merchandising can turn loyal listeners into brand ambassadors. Selling branded merchandise such as T-shirts, mugs, stickers, or tote bags can not only help spread your brand's recognition but can also serve as an additional revenue stream.

9.6. Learning Courses and Webinars

Yet another exciting path entails hosting webinars and creating learning courses based on the subject of your podcast. If your podcast delves into a specialized area of knowledge, a webinar or a learning course is a wonderful opportunity to monetize your expertise.

9.7. Affiliate Marketing

Finally, affiliate marketing presents an avenue for passive income. You can promote products from affiliate partners, and every time a sale is made through your affiliate link, you earn a commission.

Before choosing your podcast monetization strategy, remember to consider your audience, their preferences, and the niche you are in. With the right approach and a little business savvy, your podcasting endeavors can be as profitable as they are fulfilling. Just as every successful podcast is unique, so too will be its path to profitability. Embrace the versatile monetizing opportunities available to you and make your podcast not only a passion project but a prosperous enterprise!

Chapter 10. Legal Considerations for Podcasters

Podcasting is an exciting realm graced with countless opportunities for unfettered creativity. However, underneath the allure of innovation and expressiveness lay certain legal ramifications that need to be carefully understood and addressed. Before launching into the podcasting world, it's crucial to arm yourself with the knowledge and tools needed to navigate the legal landscape of this medium effectively.

10.1. Understanding Copyright Laws

In the context of podcasting, copyright infringement is an area that necessitates careful navigation. Podcast content that infringes upon the rights of a copyright owner can lead to lawsuits. Copyright laws protect original, creative works, which include music, visual arts, and even podcasts. Under this law, unauthorized use of someone else's creative work in your podcast, like playing a copyrighted song or reading verbatim from a copyrighted book without permission, could be a violation.

For this reason, always make sure to respect copyright when choosing your podcast music or guest content. There are plenty of websites offering royalty-free music specifically for podcast use. Similarly, ensure you have permission or a license to use any other form of copyrighted content in your podcast.

10.2. Fair Use Doctrine

The fair use doctrine is another key legal concept that podcasters need to understand. Fair use permits limited use of copyrighted material without the need for permission from the rights holders. Reviews, parodies, and news reporting are examples of fair use.

However, these guidelines are quite nuanced and determining whether use of a copyrighted work can be classified as 'fair use' often depends on several factors. These include purpose and character of the use, nature of the copyrighted work, the amount and substantiality of the portion used, and the effect of the use on the potential market for or value of the original work. Don't presume the notion of fair use will safeguard you in every situation; always seek legal advice when in doubt about whether your use of copyrighted material constitutes fair use.

10.3. Privacy and Defamation

Issues related to defamation and privacy are another podcasting legal aspect that requires careful consideration. If your podcast includes potentially damaging statements about individuals or companies, you may find yourself in a legal dispute over defamation.

Avoid making false factual statements that could harm someone's reputation. Equally, pay careful attention to what your guests say to avoid potential defamation claims by maintaining exclusive control over your podcast's content.

Privacy can become an issue if you disclose private facts about an individual without their consent, or if you conduct and publish an interview without the interviewee's explicit permission. Even when interviewing public figures, it is essential to respect their privacy rights and ensure they consent to the public use and distribution of the interview.

10.4. Trademark Laws

Trademark laws exist to prevent consumer confusion by making it illegal for businesses to use names or logos that are too similar to existing brands. If you use a name for your podcast that has already been trademarked by another party, you could land in trouble.

Before settling on a podcast name, consider conducting a trademark search to ensure it isn't already being used. If you find your chosen name is already being used, it may be wise to select a different name to avoid potential legal issues down the road.

10.5. Contracts

As your podcast grows, you may start to enter into contracts with guests, advertisers, and even co-hosts. Anytime you're entering into a legal agreement, it's crucial to have a clear understanding of the terms.

Contracts should spell out the rights and responsibilities of each party involved. In general, they can cover topics such as intellectual property rights, payment terms for advertisers or sponsors, and any agreed confidentiality clauses.

To avoid any potential legal misunderstandings or disputes, ensure that all contracts are reviewed by a legal professional before being signed.

10.6. Liability Insurance

Liability insurance can be the shield that protects you from lawsuits arising from the content of your podcast. Most insurance plans can cover areas such as defamation, invasion of privacy, and copyright infringement. Podcasters should evaluate the potential risks involved and consider investing in appropriate liability insurance as a protection measure.

In conclusion, while the potential legal considerations for podcasters may seem daunting, adequate research and preparation can save you potential problems. Consulting lawyers, researching copyright laws, and using insurance can effectively safeguard your journey into the podcasting world. Remember, the goal is not to scare you away from podcasting, but rather to ensure you are prepared and can confidently express your creativity without worry.

Chapter 11. Maintaining Momentum: Consistency and Growth

Momentum is more than a buzzword when it comes to podcasting. It's the beating heart of your content creation, the engine that drives engagement, and the secret to scaling your podcast. The thrill of the initial start fades, but consistency and strategic growth ensure that your lights never dim. However, how do you maintain this momentum amidst an ever-changing podcast landscape? Let's break it down.

11.1. The Essence of Consistency

Publishing consistently is perhaps the most vital key to keeping the momentum of your podcast running. Your faithful listeners will look forward to your episodes and even set their schedule around them. Therefore, it's essential to stick to a schedule and plan your content in advance.

To start, decide on a realistic routine for your podcast. If weekly episodes seem too ambitious, it's perfectly acceptable to choose a bi-weekly or monthly schedule. The most important thing is that, whatever your commitment, you honor it consistently. Utilizing podcasting scheduling tools can significantly assist in releasing content on time.

But consistency is more than just regular posting. It extends to the quality of your content. Listeners are attuned to changes in audio quality, in the way you narrate, or even the structure of your episodes. Keeping a consistent 'sound' is as important as sticking to your posting schedule. Always use the same recording setup and pre-production process to maintain your podcast's familiar 'vibe'.

11.2. Keeping Your Content Fresh

Keeping the momentum also means keeping the content original and refreshing. Sticking to consistent themes or topics will help you amass a loyal following, but experimenting with new subjects or formats can add a zest of fiesta to your podcast's staple menu.

To infuse creativity into your show, use brainstorming sessions, engage with your audience to get fresh ideas, and conduct opinion polls on future topics. Collaborate with guests who can bring diverse perspectives to your show. Using a blend of consistency and novelty will help your podcast stay captivating and relatable.

11.3. Growing Your Listener Base

Expansion is an inevitable part of longevity. So, adopting a strategic approach towards growing your listener base is paramount. Leveraging social media platforms, collaborating with fellow podcasters, or paying for targeted ads can provide you the necessary reach.

If your content is high-quality and relevant, word-of-mouth marketing will work in your favor. Encourage listener interaction through shout-outs, Q&As, contests, and reviews. Highlight user-generated content or testimonials to showcase the value you offer. Also, consider hosting live events or 'meetups' to bridge the divide between virtual and physical spaces, thus fostering intense community engagement.

11.4. Monetize and Invest Back

One of the most effective ways to maintain and build momentum is by effectively monetizing your podcast. Once your podcast begins to earn, using those funds to reinvest in your podcast can lead to exponential growth. With these finances, you could improve your content, hire a production team, or allocate more resources to marketing your podcast.

Look for sponsorship opportunities, but ensure any sponsor aligns with your theme. You could also leverage affiliate marketing or sell products related to your podcast's theme. Podcasters have also found Patreon to be a successful way to garner support from their most loyal listeners.

11.5. Staying Ahead of the Curve

The world of podcasting is continuously evolving, and staying up-to-date with the latest trends is integral to maintaining momentum. Engage with podcasting communities, learn from others' experiences, and don't hesitate to implement new ideas into your show.

Conferences and webinars offer another avenue to learn and network with a clientele you would otherwise be unable to reach. Staying connected with the latest tech developments, like voice recognition and AI, can help you adapt your content to changing listener preferences.

11.6. Coping with Podcasting Fatigue

Contrary to popular belief, podcasting is susceptible to content creator fatigue. The pressure to consistently release high-quality content, interact with listeners, manage social media, and stay ahead of trends can be daunting. However, managing these pressures is crucial for maintaining momentum.

Prioritize balanced work-life integration. Take regular breaks to prevent burnout and keep your creative juices flowing. Delegate tasks when necessary, as trying to do everything yourself may be the primary cause of your fatigue. Remember, it's your journey, and having fun while podcasting is the real secret of maintaining momentum.

In conclusion, maintaining momentum in podcasting is a blend of consistent posting, content creativity, strategic growth, monetization, staying updated, and managing fatigue. By incorporating these key elements, you'll not only maintain the momentum of your podcast but also position it for long-term success and influence. So, keep bringing the zest and sound that kept your listeners hooked in the first place, while forever pushing the envelope of innovation, progress, and excellence.